This Journal Belongs To: ____________

Made in the USA
Monee, IL
29 June 2022

98774378R00057